Alikira Richard

Online Application System - Its Weaknesses and their poss

OAS

Document Nr. V206344

Alikira Richard

Online Application System - Its Weaknesses and their possible Solutions

OAS

GRIN Verlag

Die Deutsche Bibliothek verzeichnet diese Publikation in der Deutschen Nationalbibliografie; detaillierte bibliografische Daten sind im Internet über http://dnb.d-nb.de/ abrufbar.

1. Auflage 2010
Copyright © 2010 GRIN Verlag GmbH
http://www.grin.com
Druck und Bindung: Books on Demand GmbH, Norderstedt Germany
ISBN 978-3-656-34220-5

ABSTRACT

For many years students have been applying to colleges manually. The manual Application system has made the process difficult, leading to some of the students giving up and others applying late.

The ineffectiveness of the manual Application system pushed the researchers to conduct this study so as to identify the weaknesses of manual students' Application system, identify possible solutions to the identified weaknesses. The study was carried out in Tanzania, and data was collected from four regions of Tanzania namely Dar es Salaam, Morogoro, Dodoma and Iringa. During data collection, several college students, secondary school students, registrars and parents were interviewed. It was found out that, the manual system wastes a lot of time especially when students are many. Other weaknesses included; lack of consistence, difficult in data retrieval among others. And an online Application system was seen as the only solution to the perceived problem.

PHP and MySQL were used to develop an online Application system. The system can be accessed via the web by simply typing the address of the system server in the web browser.

The major limitation of the study is that most villages have no access to the internet besides most people not being computer literate. Therefore the researcher recommends that computer lessons be made compulsory right from primary level by the government and those who cannot get access to the internet can go ahead and make use of the manual system.

TABLE OF CONTENTS

LIST OF TABLES AND FIGURES

CHAPTER ONE

INTRODUCTION

Background

According Macmillan English dictionary for advanced learners, admission is defined as a permission to join a club or become a student at a college or university.

According to Whitten and Bentley information system is an arrangement of people, data, processes, and interfaces that interact to support and improve day-to-day operations in a business as well as support the problem-solving and decision-making needs of management and users.

Online systems can provide more details and often include graphic and multimedia information for registrants. Most registration and application websites are database systems that automate the collection, tabulation and reporting of applicant information. Automated payment processing and confirmations also are standard features of online systems.

A student admission is a vital part of every college because students are what keep colleges alive. Student's admission is one of the most important activities. A poor admissions system can mean fewer students being admitted into the college because of mistakes or an overly slow response time. The process begins with a potential student completing an application form through Datastar Training college online application system service.

The next step is that, the Admissions service center reviews the application and ensures that all of the required information has been provided, from the form itself to the supplementary documentation and School certificates. If any of the required information is

missing, it is the secretary for the department to which the application concerns that contacts the potential student and arranges for the delivery of the outstanding data.

At Datastar training college, the application in its entirety is then forwarded, complete with a recommendation, to the respective department's Admissions Tutor, who has the final say as to whether each potential student is accepted or rejected. Before making a decision, the Admissions Tutor reviews the application and the additional documentation, comparing the academic credentials to a list of college rankings and previous, similar applications.

Problem Statement

The file based student Application system has for many year been very effective. However with the increase in the number of applicant, the system wastes a lot of time in terms of searching for the applicant record, in addition to requiring a large number of human resources which has led to high cost of operation. It is because of the above that an online Application system was developed to allow the organization save time and reduce on the cost of operation.

Objectives of the Study

Main Objective

The goal of the project was to develop datastar online Application system to enable applicant to apply for various courses wherever they are.

Specific Objectives

- To examine the weakness of the manual Application system at datastar training college

- To identify requirements for an on-line Application system

- To develop an on-line Application system

Research Questions

- What are the weaknesses of manual Application system.

- What are the requirements of an on-line Application system.

- What tools can be used to develop an online Application system.

Project Scope

The study was carried out at datastar training college which is found in shaurimoyo/lindi Street in Dar-es salaam. It involved identification of the weakness of the current system, requirements of an on-line Application system and tools used to develop an online Application system.

Significance

- Data search time will be reduced using the database search menus.

- The system will enhance data integrity.

- The system will help the applicants to apply for various courses via the internet (www).

CHAPTER TWO

LITERATURE REVIEW

Overview

According to Gerald(2005), a system is a set of detailed methods, procedures, and routines established or formulated to carry out a specific activity, perform a duty, or solve a problem and also could be defined as an organized, purposeful structure regarded as a whole and consisting of interrelated and interdependent elements (components, entities, factors, members, parts etc.). These elements continually influence one another (directly or indirectly) to maintain their activity and the existence of the system, in order to achieve the goal of the system.

Weaknesses of file based systems

According to Thomas & Carolyn (1998), the limitations of File-Based Approach are Separation and isolation of data, Duplication of data, Data dependence, Incompatibility of files, and Fixed queries / proliferation of application programs. Raghu & Johannes (2007) concur with Thomas & Carolyn (1998).

Separation and isolation of data: When the data is stored in separate files it becomes difficult to access. It becomes extremely complex when the data has to be retrieved from more than two files as a large amount of data has to be searched.

Duplication of data: Due to the decentralized approach, the file system leads to uncontrolled duplication of data. This is undesirable as the duplication leads to wastage of a lot

of storage space. It also costs time and money to enter the data more than once. For example, the address information of student may have to be duplicated in bus list file data.

Inconsistent Data: The data in a file system can become inconsistent if more than one person modifies the data concurrently, for example, if any student changes the residence and the change is notified to only his/her file and not to bus list. Entering wrong data is also another reason for inconsistencies.

Data dependence: The physical structure and storage of data files and records are defined in the application code. This means that it is extremely difficult to make changes to the existing structure. The programmer would have to identify all the affected programs, modify them and retest them. This characteristic of the File Based system is called program data dependence.

Incompatible File Formats: Since the structure of the files is embedded in application programs, the structure is dependent on application programming languages. Hence the structure of a file generated by COBOL programming language may be quite different from a file generated by 'C' programming language. This incompatibility makes them difficult to process jointly. The application developer may have to develop software to convert the files to some common format for processing. However, this may be time consuming and expensive.

Fixed Queries: File based systems are very much dependent on application programs. Any query or report needed by the organisation has to be developed by the application pro-

grammer. With time, the type and number of queries or reports increases. Producing different types of queries or reports is not possible in File Based Systems. As a result, in some organisations the type of queries or reports to be produced is fixed. No new query or report of the data could be generated.

Requirements of an on-line application systems

The Online application system requires the user to have a computer that is connected to the internet enable the user to access the online application database.

The online application system web application operates with the following Web Browsers: Microsoft Internet Explorer version 7.0 and above, and Mozilla Firefox 3.5 and above.

The online application system web application operates on a server running the latest versions of Apache. The Apache HTTP Server, commonly referred to as Apache, is a web server software notable for playing a key role in the initial growth of the World Wide Web. In 2009 it became the first web server software to surpass the 100 million website milestone. Apache was the first viable alternative to the Netscape Communications Corporation web server (currently named Oracle iPlanet Web Server), and since has evolved to rival other web servers in terms of functionality and performance. Typically Apache is run on a Unix-like operating system (Apache Software Foundation, 2009).

Apache is developed and maintained by an open community of developers under the auspices of the Apache Software Foundation. The application is available for a wide variety of operating systems, including Unix, GNU, FreeBSD, Linux, Solaris, Novell NetWare, AmigaOS, Mac OS X, Microsoft Windows, OS/2, TPF, and eComStation. Released under the Apache License, Apache is open-source software.

Functional Requirements

Defines about what the system must do after its successful accomplishment. Datastar online application system is able to perform these requirements, as during the requirement recitation.

The system can accept and store applicant details in the system database.

The system is able to process received from the applicants

The system is able to search a specific applicant formation from its database

The system allows the system administrator to login using user name and password.

A part from login also cans logout for security purpose.

Non Functional Requirements

According Pfaffenberger (2008), non-functional requirements refer to descriptions of the features or characteristics or attributes of a given system as well as any constraints that may limit the boundaries of the proposed solution. Whitten etal (2001) agree with Pfaffenberger by defining non-functional requirements as "constraints placed on any software project".

Tools for developing online systems

The aim of this project is to develop an interactive online application system whereby users can access using their computers connected to the internet.

The system is made up of the following two components: Database back-end and web-

based administration tool and Graphical front-end

Database back-end and web-based administration tool

The database is powered by MySQL and will be stored remotely on an Apache server at the website of the Online Application system. Storing the database remotely allows it to be updated online via a web-based interface. The web-based administration tool is written in PHP and will provide simple manipulation of the database to add, edit or delete contact information.

Graphical front-end

According to TechnologyForAll (2010) this provides an eye-catching interface to attract customers' interest to the system, and is developed using Adobe Dreamweaver CS3. Dreamweaver is an application used for creating interactive WebPages that communicate with remote databases. It allows a great level of customization in layout, animation and scripting content – a level of which isn't available in many other application environments. The front-end displays contact information retrieved from the database back-end, which updates at regular intervals. This is something which Dreamweaver has helped the researchers accomplish with the use of animation, video content and an attractive design.

CHAPTER THREE

METHODOLOGY

This chapter presents tools, techniques, and methodologies that will be used to develop the system. It covers the research design, the study population, sample size, research instruments that will be used, procedure for data collection among others.

Research Design

To develop a manageable specification of the proposed system, a study using questionnaires and interviews were used to collect data from various colleges including darstar from College Students, Students registries, Form 6 students, form 4 students and parents. Purposive sampling was used to select the parents and registrars whereas random sampling will be used to select students.

Execution of the situation analysis is arranged such that it started with the expression of the objectives of the study which is in line with project expectations (demand). The core purpose of the analysis was to obtain relevant information and data from various research areas that will form the basis for the development of an on-line Application system.

This particular study involves views of the validity of the current project with respect to market and its requirements in general

- Identification of weakness of manual online Application system by students, registrars and parents in the current and future.
- Assessing how many people can use the internet from our sample study for the proposed system.
- The percentage will opt for implementation of the new online Application system.

Study Population

The study area covered the following areas: College Students, Students registrars, Form 6 students, form 4 students and their parents from Datastar Training College, Mororogo (sokoine university Agriculture and Mzumbe University), Mwanza (St. Augustine

University), Dodoma(CBE-Dodoma and Chamwino Secondary School), Iringa(Mkwawa University college, Lugalo Secondary School and Highland Secondary School). The total population was 200 and we decided to narrow it 50 for more accuracy.

Sample Size

A Sample size of fifty people was taken. Purposive sampling technique was employed to select the sample. The fifty selected people included: fifteen college students, five student registrars, fifteen form six students, ten form four students, and five parents.

Sampling Procedure

The purpose was to collect information that is essential to a wider area. To that effect purposive sampling technique was utilized in order to draw a relevant sample for the present study, in this account various College Students, Students registrars, Form 6 students, form 4 students and parents questioned.

Data Collection Instrument

Questionnaire and interviews were subjected to individuals College Students, Students registrars, Form 6 students, form 4 students and parents. We used questionnaires because it provided for us an inexpensive means for gathering data from a large number of individuals and interview allowed interviewee to respond freely and openly to questions and we established a good rapport.

Data collection Procedure

The researchers started collecting data within the districts of Dar es Salaam in the first

seven days of the research. They interviewed five college students, two registrars of students, eight secondary school students and two parents.

Then on the eighth and nineth days, the researchers travelled to Morogoro where interviews were conducted with two students of Sokoine University of Agriculture, one student of Mzumbe University and one student of St. Augustine University of Tanzania. The researchers then interviewed the registrar of St. Augustine University of Tanzania. On the tenth and eleventh days, the researchers interviewed four form six students and two form four students of Mzumbe Secondary School. The researchers further interviewed one parent.

Day twelve found the researchers on their way to Dodoma where they spent day thirteen and fourteen interviewing three students of the College of Business Education (CBE - Dodoma) and their registrar. The researchers then interviewed two form four students of Chamwino Secondary School, four form six students and one parent.

The researchers spent day fifteen travelling to Iringa where they interviewed three students of University of Dar es Salaam – Mkwawa University College of Education (MUCE) and their registrar on the sixteenth day of their research. On the following day, the researchers interviewed three form six students of Lugalo Secondary School, two students of Highland Secondary school and one parent.

Data Analysis

The data collected from all those places were then analyzed to enable the researches identify the weaknesses of the manual Application System, gather requirements of the online Application System, and use them for the development stage of the proposed

system.

CHAPTER FOUR

DATA ANALYSIS AND INTERPRETATION

Data Analysis

The data collected from fifty people in the selected research areas gave us a wide knowledge on the online Application system and it has helped us to know limitations of existing manual system. Below is the table showing the results of the questionnaires.

Research Area	Number of Respondents	Number of respondents who accepted the manual system has a problem	Number of respondents with knowledge of the internet	Number of respondents who opted for an online system
College Students	15	15	15	13
Student Registrars	5	3	4	3
Form 6 Students	15	10	12	9
Form 4 Students	10	5	6	4
Parents	5	4	3	3
TOTALS	50	37	40	32
PERCENTAGE (%)	100	74	80	64

FIGURE 4.1: Table of Statistical Data

The data presented in Figure 4.1 above shows how different research areas of respondents have opted for implementation of an online Application system as stipulated

in the table above. The table shows a higher number of respondents who accepted that; using a manual system is a time consuming task during Application processes. Another exercise was to get number of Internet users as per our sample size, before concluding with the number of people suggesting the development of an online Application system.

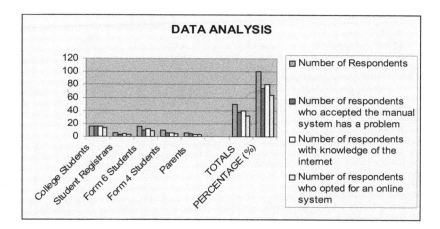

Figure 4.2: Graph Representation of the Statistical Data

INTERPRETATION

The findings presented in Figures 4.1 & 4.2 above show that over 74% of the people from the questionnaire have accepted there is a problem using a manual Application system but only 26% preferred the continuity of a manual system proving a number of reason such as "this is a new system it will take time people to adopt especially those in rural areas where the internet services are unavailable", but a bigger number of respondents preferred an online Application system to be implemented.

Figure 4.1 shows that 80% of the respondents use internet in one way or another, as presented on our research areas. This makes internet an ideal media for the new online Application system which is available 24hrs a day even when the application college offices

are closed, yet also cheaper for people who are far away from the college they need not to travel to bring their applications.

Figures 4.1 & 4.2 also show that 64% of all the respondents suggested for the development of the online Application system. This made the researchers see the true need of having this system in place and hence developing it to eliminate the weaknesses pointed out in the manual Application system.

SYSTEM ENVIRONMENT

The System Environment of the Datastar online application information system is as follows

Hardware Environment:

Processor   : At list 1.6 MHZ

Hard disk   : At list 60 GB

RAM   : At list 1 GB

Operating System   : Window 7 or windows xp.

Database   : MYSQL Database Management system.

TECHNOLOGIES AND SOFTWARE USED.

The technology used to develop Data star online application information system

PHP scripting LANGUAGE

MYSQL database management.

SOFTWARE USED

MACROMEDIA DREAMWEAVER, which is used to design the HTML pages, forms and   PHP scripts

STAR UML this is used for data modeling

CHAPTER FIVE

SYSTEM DESIGN

Designing of the online Application system underwent two major stages: - The Logical Design, and the Physical Design.

Logical Design

According to Garry & Harry (2011), the logical design of a system pertains to an abstract representation of the data flows, inputs and outputs of the system. This is often conducted via modeling, using an over-abstract (and sometimes graphical) model of the actual system. The logical design specifies the main methods of interaction in terms of menu structures and command structures.

There exist number of frameworks for structuring, controlling and   planning the development of an information system.the methodology used to develop Datastar online Application system has enhanced waterfall model of development as stated by, as stated

by Roger,(2005), is used when the requirements of a problem are reasonably well understood, methodology chosen is based on the following facts

This project has clear objectives and solution.

Project requirements can be stated unambiguously and comprehensively.

With enhanced waterfall methodology, a project is divided into sequential phases with some overlap and splash back acceptable between phases.

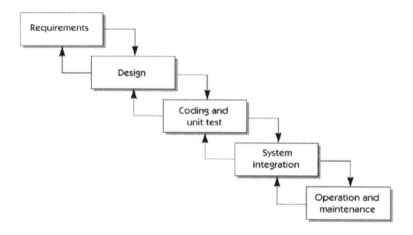

Figure 5.1: Enhanced waterfall model used for software development

Use Case Diagram

The use-case diagram is a model of the system's intended functions and its environment. It is used as an essential input to activities in analysis, design, and test or it simply outlining the system's functionality and delimiting the system; for example, establishing what actors and use cases exist, and how they interact. The most important purpose of a use-case model is to communicate the system's behavior to the end user. Actors help

delimit the system and give a clearer picture of what it is supposed to do. Use cases are developed on the basis of the actors' needs. This ensures that the system will turn out to be what the users expected.

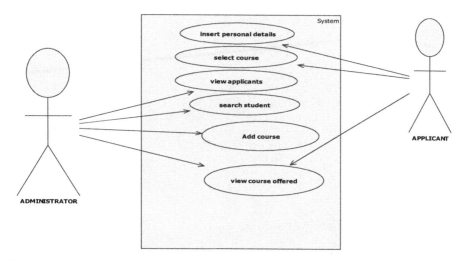

Figure 5.2.Use case diagram for data star online application information system

Context diagram

Context diagram for data star online application information system boundaries, external entities that interact with the system, and major information flows between entities and the system itself.

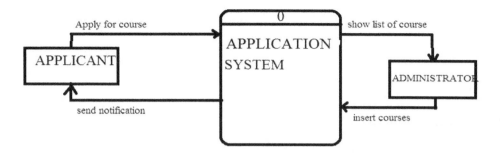

Figure 5.3: Context diagram for data star online Application system

DATA FLOW DIAGRAM (DFD)

The developed data star online Application system

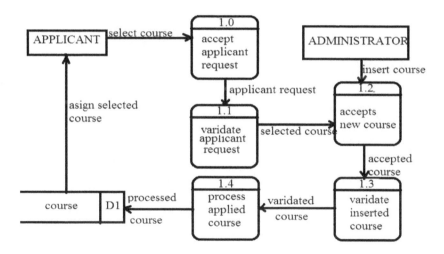

Figure 5.4: Data Flow for data star online Application system.

Conceptual database design

Conceptual database design involves modeling the collected information at a high-level of abstraction without using a particular data model or DBMS.

Entities identified from the data requirements

APPLICANT (AppId   LastName, MiddleName, FirstName, gender,

MobileNumber, email, EducationLevel, division)

COURSE (CourseCode, CourseName, duration)

ENTITY RELATIONSHIP DIAGRAM (ERD)

An Entity relationship diagram is a specialized graphic that illustrates the relationship between entities in a database. The type of relationship used in during developing the database for data star online course application information system is one to many. This means that one course can be applied by many students.

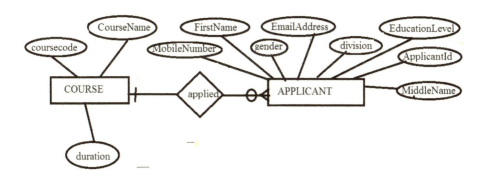

Figure 5.5: Entity relationship diagram.

KEY INTEGRITY

A UNIQUE key integrity constraint requires that every value in a column or set of columns (key) be unique--that is, no two rows of a table have duplicate values in a specified column or set of columns.

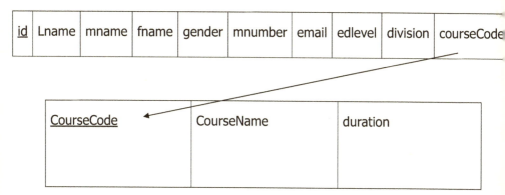

id	Lname	mname	fname	gender	mnumber	email	edlevel	division	courseCode

CourseCode	CourseName	duration

Figure 5.6: Reverential integrity

USER AND SYSTEM REQUIREMENT APPLICANT

The applicants will interact directly with the system by inserting his or her personal details, such as last name, middle name, first name, gender, mobile number, email address, education level, division and lastly select the course want to study. The applicants will be required either to upload there relevant certificates through the colleges email address or submit the hard copy for more verification eligible applicants to various course.

Physical Design

In this phase, the team completes the technical blueprints for the new system, based on the implementation platform.

According to Rosenblatt (2011), states physical design is the actual input and output

processes of the system. This is laid down in terms of how data is input into a system, how it is verified or authenticated, how it is processed, and how it is displayed as output.

The datarstar online Application system consists of user interfaces that enable the users to interact with the system. A system has the interfaces for the applicants that will enable them to insert personal details and select the course of their choice.

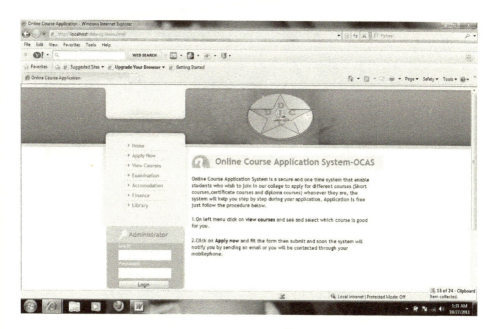

Figure 5.7: Table, Shows a home page which gives instruction to the applicant

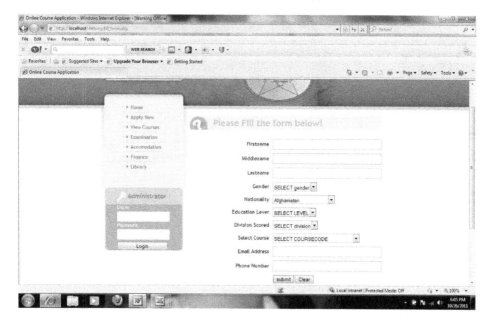

Figure 5.8: Table, shows when an applicant is applying for any course

The datastar online Application system has also interfaces that enable the system administrator to interact with the system. System administrator is needed to login first before any access is done.

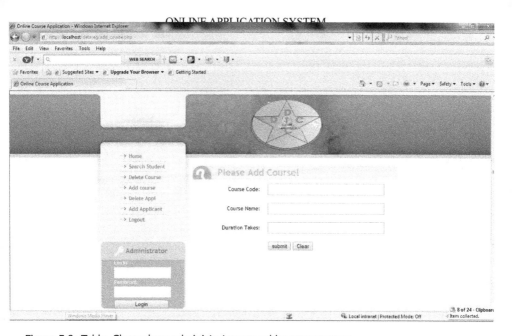

Figure 5.9: Table, Shows how administrator can add a new courses

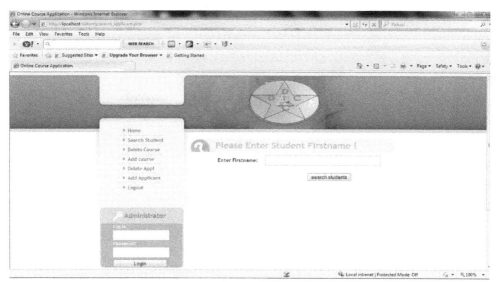

Figure 5.10: Table, Shows how to search for a student who has already applied for the course.

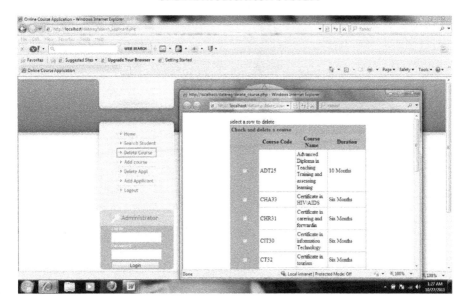

Figure 5.11:Shows how to deleting a course which opens a new window

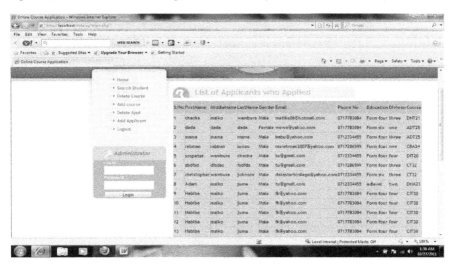

Figure 5.12: table, shows list of applicants who applied using online system.

CHAPTER SIX:

FINDINGS, CONCLUTIONS AND RECOMMENDATIONS

Findings

From the research conducted on the online Application system, following the objectives of the study, the following were the key findings: -

According to objective one of this study, the following are the weaknesses of the manual Application system. Its time consuming exercise which is more prone to human error and paper work is tedious such that the filling, filing, storage and retrieval of the registry information becomes drudgery.

Again, according to the second objective of this study, the requirements of the online Application system it was discovered that internet is the ideal medium of communication to be used by the new online Application system.

According to objective three flowcharts, Data Flow Diagrams, Context Diagrams and Entity Relationship Diagrams are the best tools to use in designing an online Application system that will collect, store, maintain applicants information for ease of access by using the internet, that makes it very user-friendly and therefore anyone with just little knowledge of using the internet can use it.

Conclusions

According to the first objective, the weaknesses of the manual Application System make it very ineffective. It is very difficult to use the manual system now that the number of applying students is rising every year.

According to the second objective, the requirements gathered for the Online Application System prove that this system can be more efficient than the manual system.

According to the third objective, designing the Online Application System has proves to be less costly and it takes little time as also application of the system saves time.

Recommendations

According to the first objective, the manual Application system should be replaced by the Online Application System considering the weaknesses it has proved to have.

According to the second objective, the requirements gathered are necessary for creating the Online Application System and will make it a more efficient system compared to the manual system.

According to the third objective, the tools used to design an Online Application System are the best tools as they make it easy to develop an efficient online system of Application that saves time and can easily be accessed by many applicants at the same time.

REFERENCES

- Lewis,J.P (1995).*Fundamental of project management*, New York: American management association

- Lewis,J.P(1995b) *Project planning,scheduling and control* (Rev.ed).Chicago :IRWIN Professional publication .

- Gerald V.post(2005):*Database Management System*(Third Edition) Newyork: McGraw Hill

- Hoffer ,J.,Georg J.,Valancin,J,Panigrahi,P(2006),*Modern System Analysis and Designing*

- Dorling Kindersley India Bruegge,B,Dutoit, A (2002),*Object Oriented Software Engineering*: Conquering Complex and changing Systems,New Jesey,Prentience Hall Inc.

- Avision,D.,Firtzgerald,G.(1997),*Information System Development: Methodologies Techniques and Tools*, Great Britain:McGrae-Hill.

- Jeffrey, L., Lonnie, D. & Kevin, B.(2001). *Systems analysis and design methods*. (5th Ed.)Newyork: McGraw-Hill.

- Macmillan Education,(2007).*Macmillan English dictionary for advanced learners*(2nd Ed.)Martin Shovel: Macmillan Publishers Ltd.

- Apache Software Foundation. (2009). Project Listings: *Apache Software Foundation*. Retrieved October 22, 2011, from Apache Software Foundation:

- Rosenblatt, G. B. (2011). *Systems Analysis and Design* (9th Ed.) Boston: Course Technology.

- Thomas, C. & Carolyn, B. (1998), *Database Systems: A Practical Approach to Design, Implementation, and Management,* 2nd edition, Adson W.sley, New York.

- TechnologyForAll.(2008, May). *Dreamweaver Designing Tutorial: TechnologyForAll.* Retrieved October 24, 2011, from TechnologyForAll:

- *http://www.ehow.com/facts_6891377_use-online-registration_.html*

QUESTIONNAIRE

PREAMBLE:

We are students at KIU university-dar es salaam. As one of the prerequisite requirement for the award of a degree of information technology every student is required to undertake a study in an area of his/her interest with the aim of demonstrating his ability to carry out and manage a project. Our study title is "online Application system a case in datastar training college" Kindly assist us by completing this document. The information you provide will not be used for other purpose other than study and for academic use only.

1. What category are you?

College student   [ ]

Form 6 student   [ ]

Form 4 student   [ ]

Registrars   [ ]

Parent   [ ]

Others...

2. What is your view of manual Application system?

Good   [ ]

Poor   [ ]

Please give reasons...

....

....

3. Do you have the knowledge of the internet?

Yes   [   ]   No   [   ]

4. Do you think an on-line Application system is preferable to manual Application system?

Yes   [   ]   No   [   ]

Please give reasons...

....

....

With great thanks